THE SECOND MISSIONARY JOURNEY OF PAUL
(A Study in Missions)

REVISED

Dr. Dan S. Bailey

Search
the
Scriptures
Ministries

Rev. Dan S. Bailey
646 Liberty Hill Road * Hartwell, GA 30643

ISBN: 9798860401303

Independently published

DEDICATION

To all those who are praying about doing more for the Lord!
For those precious souls who are labouring in the mission
fields of the world. To the Missionaries that have
surrendered their lives to carry the gospel message.

These lessons will require a desire to learn more about missions. In order to do these lessons, you will need a King James Version of the Bible, a desire to study and to learn more about the Word of God, and diligence in doing the lessons. I pray these studies will enrich your life and cause you to be a better servant for the Lord!

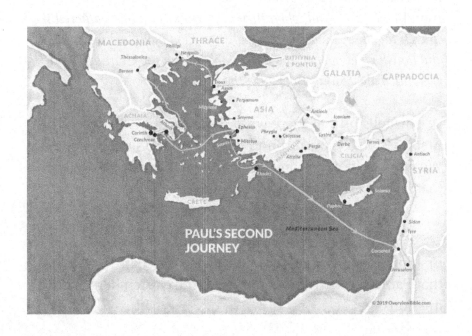

Lesson One:
Between the Two Journeys

Remember that Acts 14 had ended with these two verses. Acts 14:27, 28, *"And when they were come, and had gathered the church together, they rehearsed all that God had done with them, and how he had opened the door of faith unto the Gentiles. And there they abode long time with the disciples."*

This tells us that there was a period of time between the first missionary journey and the second missionary journey. We want to look at some of the things the Scripture tells us that happened during this time.

No doubt they were rejoicing because of the success of the first missionary journey. I believe also that there was a lot that Paul and Barnabas could teach the church here about missions.

Acts 15:1 says, *"And certain men which came down from Judaea taught the brethren, and said, Except ye be circumcised after the manner of Moses, ye cannot be saved."*

This chapter records the first general council of the newly instituted church in Jerusalem. We are told they are called together because of a dispute among some of the leaders of the church of Jerusalem concerning circumcision being essential for a Gentile to be saved. Dr. Sightler says that we find in the church in Galatia, some Jewish believers who came to the Galatian believes and insisted they be circumcised after the custom of the Law of Moses in order to be a Gentile believer in the Lord Jesus Christ. Paul disputed with them and stated that their salvation was based entirely upon the matter of faith, a personal faith in the Lord Jesus without the deeds of the law and without the rite of Jewish circumcision. He told them that the Gentiles were not required to be circumcised in order to be a disciple of the Lord Jesus.

Paul makes mention of this in his letter to the Galatians in chapters 1 and 2. These men that had come down said, *"Except ye be circumcised after the manner of Moses, ye cannot be saved."* What they said is that, you say you are a Christian, but without circumcision, we do not accept you as a follower of Christ. This was a disturbing statement and one that must be cleared up because of the Gentiles that had accepted Christ many other Gentiles that would be saved.

Dr. Criswell says, "What they are saying is: A man cannot be saved by trusting Jesus alone. In order to be saved, one must trust Jesus, and he must do something else."

Paul had written to the Galatians in chapter 5:2, 4, 6 and said,
"Behold, I Paul say unto you, that if ye be Circumcised ,

Christ shall profit you nothing .

Christ *is become of no effect unto you, whosoever*

of you are ___justified___ *by the law; ye are fallen from*

___grace___ *. For in Jesus Christ neither* ___circumcision___

availeth any thing, nor ___uncircumcision___ *; but*

___faith___ *which worketh by* ___love___ *."*

Acts 15:2 says, *"When therefore Paul and Barnabas had no small dissension and disputation with them, they determined that Paul and Barnabas, and certain other of them, should go up to Jerusalem unto the apostles and elders about this question."*

The *"they"* mentioned in verse 2 is referring to the church at Antioch. They determined that they would go to Jerusalem and get this matter settled once and for all. This was important to the Gentiles saved in Antioch and Galatia and Jerusalem and all of Paul's newly instituted congregations. So the church sends Paul and Barnabas along with several others, up to Jerusalem to debate the question and to get it settled finally and completely.

Acts 15:3, 4 says, *"And being brought on their way by the church, they passed through Phenice and Samaria, declaring the conversion of the Gentiles: and they caused great joy unto all the brethren. And when they were come to Jerusalem, they were received of the church, and of the apostles and elders, and they declared all things that God had done with them."*

It says in verse 3 that they were brought on their way by the church, which means that they were taken care of by the church. All their expenses were taken care of by the church. I'm sure there were a lot of financial expense in their journey as well as many spiritual needs they would face. The church knew that it was important to the life of the church that this problem be taken care of. If they were to continue to prosper, this issue concerning salvation had to be settled. We should be mindful of the weight of the burden that the missionary carries today. <u>We should be able to help them both financially and spiritually in their labors.</u>

As they passed through Phenice and Samaria they preached the conversion of the Gentiles which caused great joy to all the brethren. When they came into Jerusalem they were received, first of all by the church and then by the apostles and elders who were members of the church. Here they reported to the church all that the Lord had done with them. Their testimony alone of the many Gentiles that had been saved on the first missionary journey should have been sufficient to settle the matter they had come to debate.

Acts 15:5-6 says, *"But there rose up certain of the sect of the*

Pharisees *which believed, saying, That it was*

needful *to circumcise them, and to* **command**

them to **Keep** *the* **law** **of** **Moses** *. And the*

apostles and elders came together for to consider of this matter."

Notice the problem was from a sect of the Pharisees that was saying circumcision was necessary for a person to be saved. This was a group of Pharisees it is said "which believed." Apparently they believed the wrong thing in order to be saved.

Jesus and the early Church had a number of conflicts with the Pharisees. Read Matthew 23 to understand better what Jesus thought of their teaching. Jesus called them "blind guides" in verse 16. He called them fools in verse 17. In verse 27, He says they are like whited sepulchers, full of dead men's bones, and all uncleanness. He calls them serpents in verse 33 and also refers to them as a generation of vipers.

To be able to see some of the wrong teachings of the Pharisees consider the Pharisee's meticulous approach to Sabbath-keeping, they really stand out as an interesting case study in how religion can be done wrong. Here is a list of a few of their Sabbath traditions:

The Pharisees didn't permit people to carry mats about on the Sabbath. John chapter 5 tells us about how Jesus permitted a man He had just healed to carry his mat. The Pharisees focused more on the fact that one of their traditions were broken than that a person was miraculously healed!

They also didn't permit people to carry clothing with them on the Sabbath, unless they were wearing it. If a person's house caught fire on the Sabbath, a person wouldn't have been allowed to save an article of clothing by carrying it out. However, they were permitted to put on as much clothing as they could and leave their house with what they were wearing!

They also didn't permit people to carry metal around with them on the Sabbath. The nails that were in a person's shoes were included in the prohibition, so many people had special Sabbath footwear!

They considered spitting on the ground a no-no on the Sabbath. The reasoning was that plowing was a kind of work, and they defined "plowing" as any act that disturbed the ground, even slightly. And, as they saw it, the slight disturbance caused by spitting was enough to be considered work!

The Pharisees only permitted people to travel a certain distance from their home on the Sabbath. They also defined their home as where their doorpost was located, so some of them removed their doorpost from its place and took it with them, and in so doing, they were permitted to travel as far as they wished on the Sabbath. Not only did they develop their own traditions, they developed their own work-arounds! (https://truthsower.wordpress.com/2019/11/02/the-pharisees-a-case-study-in-religion-gone-wrong/)

* Who were the "they" referred to in Acts 15:2?

The church in Antioch

* What did "being brought on their way" in Acts 15:3 mean?

Cared for by the church

* In what 2 ways should we be able to help the missionaries?
1. Financially
2. Spiritually

Lesson Two:
The Councils Decision

Verse 6 tells us that the apostles and elders came together to consider the matter. They were trying to nail down once and for all just how men were to be saved. Were the Gentiles to be saved the same way the Jews were. Was it supposed to be by faith or were they to add the works of the law to salvation? This was the question they were to discuss and what a powerful question it was.

Matthew Henry says that they did not come to give their separate judgments on the subject, but came together to . . . hear one another's sense in this matter. He says, for in the multitude of counsellors there is safety.

Acts 15:7 – 11 says, "*And when there had been much*

_____, Peter rose up, and said unto them, Men

and brethren, ye know how that a good while ago God made choice

among us, that the _____ by my mouth should

hear the word of the _____, and _____.

And God, which knoweth the hearts, bare them witness, giving

them the Holy Ghost, even as he did unto us; And put no

_____ between us and them, purifying their

hearts by _____. Now therefore why tempt ye God, to

put a yoke upon the neck of the disciples, which neither our

fathers nor we were able to bear? But we believe that through the

_____ of the Lord _____ Christ we shall be

_____, even as they."

When Peter speaks he is giving testimony of what took place in the house of Cornelius. It was here that God allowed Peter to preach the gospel to the Gentile household of Cornelius and as the Holy Spirit fell on the congregation and they repented and received Christ. Peter knew that what he did there was of God. He was assured that nothing else was needed for these Gentiles to be saved other that what they had received. Peter saw no reason for them to yoke the Gentiles with something that he says, *"neither our fathers nor we were able to bear."* Peter declared that salvation comes to the Jew and the Gentile through the grace of the Lord Jesus Christ.

Then as the counsel is quietly considering this testimony, Paul and Barnabas stand up to speak. Acts 15:12 says *"Then all the multitude kept silence, and gave audience to Barnabas and Paul, declaring what miracles and wonders God had wrought among the Gentiles by them."* They begin to again rehearse before those present the miracles and wonders that God had done to the Gentiles by their preaching to them. Testimony after testimony of those Gentiles that had been gloriously saved by Paul and Barnabas simply preaching Christ to them. There was no doubt in Paul and Barnabas's mind that

God's way of salvation was "by grace through faith in Jesus Christ". Everything that was needed to be done for a person, Jew or Gentile, to be saved was done by Christ on the cross. All they needed to do was believe in the finished work of Christ, repent of their sins and accept His grace that had been extended to them.

James now, as moderator of this council, decides there has been enough testimony and steps forth to speak. Acts 15:13-21 says, *"And after they had held their peace, James answered, saying, Men and brethren, hearken unto me: Simeon hath declared how God at the first did visit the Gentiles, to take out of them a people for his name. And to this agree the words of the prophets; as it is written, After this I will return, and will build again the tabernacle of David, which is fallen down; and I will build again the ruins thereof, and I will set it up: That the residue of men might seek after the Lord, and all the Gentiles, upon whom my name is called, saith the Lord, who doeth all these things. Known unto God are all his works from the beginning of the world. Wherefore my sentence is, that we trouble not them, which from among the Gentiles are turned to God: But that we write unto them, that they abstain from pollutions of idols, and from fornication, and from things strangled, and from blood. For Moses of old time hath in every city them that preach him, being read in the synagogues every sabbath day."*

He reminds them further of the testimony of Simeon who said that God would visit the Gentiles and take out of them a people for His name. Then he refers to the account of the prophets who declared the salvation of the Gentiles. And then James declares that the will and plan of God has been written and known from the beginning of the world. Upon these testimonies James then declares his sentence in the matter before them. He said that the Gentiles were not to be troubled with the thought of having to be circumcised to be saved. That faith in the grace of God was enough. He did declare also that the Gentiles were to be reminded to abstain from pollutions of idols and from fornication and from things strangled and from blood. That is to say, they were to keep themselves pure from the defilements of this old world.

In Acts 15:22-30 it is said, *"Then pleased it the apostles and elders, with the whole church, to send chosen men of their own company to Antioch with Paul and Barnabas; namely, Judas surnamed Barsabas, and Silas, chief men among the brethren: And they wrote letters by them after this manner; The apostles and elders and brethren send greeting unto the brethren which are of the Gentiles in Antioch and Syria and Cilicia: Forasmuch as we have heard, that certain which went out from us have troubled you with words, subverting your souls, saying, Ye must be circumcised, and keep the law: to whom we gave no such commandment: It seemed good unto us, being assembled with one accord, to send chosen men unto you with our beloved Barnabas and Paul, Men that have hazarded their lives for the name of our Lord Jesus Christ. We have sent therefore Judas and Silas, who shall also tell you the same things by mouth. For it seemed good to the Holy Ghost, and to us, to lay upon you no greater burden than these necessary things; That ye abstain from meats offered to idols, and from blood, and from things strangled, and from fornication: from which if ye keep yourselves, ye shall do well. Fare ye well. So when they were dismissed, they came to Antioch: and when they had gathered the multitude together, they delivered the epistle:"*

The apostles and elders and the whole church were pleased to send Judas surnamed Barsabas and Silas to Antioch with Paul and Barnabas with letters declaring to the Gentiles the decision made by the council at Jerusalem. They wanted the Gentiles to know that the teaching that certain men had been teaching concerning the need for circumcision to be saved, was not authorized by them. These two men along with the letters from the council were sent with Paul and Barnabas to verify that this indeed was the final word from the council on this matter.

They had no doubt great respect for Paul and Barnabas saying that they were men "that have hazarded their lives for the name of our Lord Jesus Christ. Verse 30 tells us that when they came to Antioch and had gathered the multitude together they delivered this letter from the council.

Acts 15:31 - 34 says, *"Which when they had read, they rejoiced for the consolation. And Judas and Silas, being prophets also themselves, exhorted the brethren with many words, and confirmed them. And after they had tarried there a space, they were let go in peace from the brethren unto the apostles. Notwithstanding it pleased Silas to abide there still."*

Rejoicing and confirmation is made among the Church and then these men, Judas and Silas, were released from their charge and were allowed to go back to Jerusalem. But Silas decides to stay in Antioch.

   * **When Peter speaks, he is giving testimony of what happened in what place?**

   * **How does Peter declare that salvation comes to the Jew and the Gentile?**

* What did Paul and Barnabas think was God's way of salvation?

* What was James' judgment on the matter of salvation for the Gentiles?

* What 2 men were sent from Jerusalem to Antioch with Paul and Barnabas?

* Which one of these men decides to stay in Antioch?

Lesson Three:
Beginning the Second Journey

Acts 15: 35 – 40 says, *"Paul also and Barnabas continued in Antioch, teaching and preaching the word of the Lord, with many others also. And some days after Paul said unto Barnabas, Let us*

go _____ *and visit our* _____ *in* _____

city where we have _____ *the* _____

of the Lord, and see _____ *they do. And Barnabas determined to take with them John, whose surname was Mark. But Paul thought not good to take him with them, who departed from them from Pamphylia, and went not with them to the work. And the contention was so sharp between them, that they departed asunder one from the other: and so Barnabas took Mark, and sailed unto Cyprus; And Paul chose Silas, and departed, being recommended by the brethren unto the grace of God. And he went through Syria and Cilicia, confirming the churches."*

We are told that Paul and Barnabas continued to teach and preach the word of the Lord in Antioch along with many others. And then came the day when Paul told Barnabas that it was time for them <u>to visit the brethren in the cities where they had already preached the word in their first missionary journey</u>. The purpose being to check on how these believers were doing.

CONTENTION BETWEEN PAUL AND BARNABAS

Barnabas was determined that John Mark was going to go on this journey with them, but Paul didn't think that was a good idea. Paul was remembering that John Mark had left them in their first missionary journey and was not sure that he would be able or beneficial to them on this journey. The contention was so strong that these two great men had to part their ways. Barnabas took John Mark and sailed to Cyprus, his home country, while Paul took Silas and went through Syria and Cilicia, his home country, confirming the churches. The churches approval was apparently on Paul and Silas and they recommended them unto the grace of God.

Lest we think bad of John Mark, who was the writer of the Gospel of Mark, Paul just didn't think that he was as fervent in the ministry as he should be. Barnabas, on the other-hand, is known as the son of consolation and thought it to be a good idea to give Mark a second chance.

One lesson from verse 39 that Dr. Sightler points out is "that when contentions come, or difference of opinions might flair up, there is no indication in such, no reason why a man should break fellowship, not at all. We will agree and we shall disagree; but we will resolve and purpose by the grace of God to love one another in spite of disagreements. . . I am inclined to believe it to be God's will for Paul to revisit these churches. But it was also God's will for Barnabas to go to his own country, Cyprus, with Mark and do a mission work there."

Later Paul had a better opinion of Mark for he writes to

Timothy in 2 Timothy 4:11, *"Take Mark and bring him with thee, for he is profitable to me for the ministry."* And in Colossians 4:10 he mentions *". . .Marcus, sister's son to Barnabas, (touching whom ye received commandments: if he come unto you, receive him;)"*

AT DERBE AND LYSTRA – INTRODUCTION TO TIMOTHY

In Acts 16:1 – 5 we are told, *"Then came he to Derbe and Lystra: and, behold, a certain disciple was there, named Timotheus, the son of a certain woman, which was a Jewess, and believed; but his father was a Greek: Which was well reported of by the brethren that were at Lystra and Iconium. Him would Paul have to go forth with him; and took and circumcised him because of the Jews which were in those quarters: for they knew all that his father was a Greek. And as they went through the cities, they delivered them the decrees for to keep, that were ordained of the apostles and elders which were at Jerusalem. And so were the churches established in the faith, and increased in number daily."*

One of the first places mentioned that Paul and Silas came to was Derbe and Lystra. Paul and Barnabas had preached in these places before on their first missionary journey and had left many believers there. We are introduced here to a disciple by the name of <u>Timotheus. He is the son of a Jewess woman who believed and a Greek father</u>. We are told that he was well reported of by the brethren here. We know Timothy from the two letters that Paul would later write to him, 1 & 2 Timothy. Here Paul chooses Timothy to go with him and Silas. Paul had Timothy circumcised because of the Jews there that all knew his father was a Greek. This is a different situation than what was dealt with at the council in

Jerusalem in chapter 15. Here is a man that is a believer, but he is mixture of Jew and Gentile blood. It seems that not as a means of compromise, but rather for his testimonies sake, Paul decided it best that Timothy be circumcised.

As they were revisiting the churches they had started in the first missionary journey, they delivered to them the letters that had come from the Jerusalem council. These churches were <u>said to be established in the faith</u>, meaning that they were solid in their standing for Christ. Also they were growing churches for verse 5 tells us <u>they were increasing in number daily.</u>

* **What was the purpose of the second missionary journey?**

* **What was the contention between Paul and Barnabas all about?**

* **Where did Barnabas and John Mark go?**

* **Where did Paul and Silas go?**

* **According to Dr. Sightler, was it God's will for Barnabas to go to Cyprus?**

* **Did Paul ever have a different opinion of John Mark?**

* Who are we introduced to in Acts 16:1? What was different about him?

* What 2 things are said about the churches that Paul and Silas visited?

1.

2.

Lesson Four:
From Phrygia to Philippi

IN PHRYGIA, GALATIA, THEN FORBIDDEN TO PREACH IN
ASIA. IN MYSIA, FORBIDDEN TO GO TO BITHYNIA.
FROM MYSIA TO TROAS WHERE PAUL HAS A VISION.
THEY LEFT TROAS AND WENT TO SAMOTHRACIA.
THEN THE NEXT DAY TO NEAPOLIS THEN TO PHILIPPI.

Acts 16:6 - 12 says *"Now when they had gone throughout*

Phrygia and the region of Galatia, and were _____ *of*

the _____ _____ *to preach the word in*

_____, *After they were come to Mysia, they assayed to go*

into _____ : *but the* _____ *suffered them*

not. And they passing by Mysia came down to _____. *And*

a _____ *appeared to Paul in the night; There stood a man*

of _____, *and prayed him, saying,* _____

_____ *into Macedonia, and* _____ *us. And after he*

had seen the vision, _____ *we endeavored to*

_____ *into Macedonia,* _____ *gathering that the*

Lord had _____ us for to _____ the

_____ unto them. Therefore loosing from Troas, we came with a straight course to Samothracia, and the next day to Neapolis; And from thence to Philippi, which is the chief city of that part of Macedonia, and a colony: and we were in that city abiding certain days."

This is a particularly special portion of Scripture to me, for it was this passage of the Word of God that the Lord used in getting me involved in missions many years ago. This is known as "The Macedonian call". Several things to notice here before we get to that though. First of all, we see that they had gone throughout Phrygia and the region of Galatia, but then the verse tells us they were "forbidden of the Holy Ghost" to preach the word <u>in Asia</u>". <u>We see the leading of the Holy Spirit in their ministry.</u> They were going into Asia to preach the Gospel message, but the Holy Spirit said no. They then went to Mysia and planned to go <u>into Bithynia</u>, but again the Spirit would not let them.

If you have never been led by the Spirit in this way, you are missing a real blessing. I believe they prayed about where the Lord wanted them to go next and that day by day as they preached the Word, the Spirit of God was leading them to the place He wanted them to be. That's the way many of our missionaries on the field around the world today found where God wanted them to be. <u>First of all, you need to be preaching the Word where you are and then begin praying where else the Lord might let you preach!</u> Don't ever expect to find the will of God for your life by sitting and doing nothing. If you won't tell people here about the Lord Jesus Christ, don't expect Him to send you to the other side of the world to minister. If you're not doing it here, you won't do it there!

Dr. Sightler tells us why they were not allowed to go to these places that the Holy Spirit forbid them to go. He said, "the reason is not because God did not desire the word be preached, but rather, the Lord had a better alternative, including the Macedonian call which would call Paul and Silas away from Israel, even up into the continent of Europe to tell the story to barbaric people who lived on the continent of Europe two thousand years ago." Many times in our lives, if we will let the Holy Spirit be our Guide, we will find that He will lead us to places where we are most needed, instead of the places that we want to go.

As they passed by Mysia they came down to Troas, where Paul had a vision in the night. The thing he saw was a man of Macedonia, and he was saying "Come over into Macedonia and help us." The verse tells us that immediately after he had seen the vision they endeavored to go into Macedonia and the scripture tells us of their assurance of their call, "assuredly gathering that the Lord had called us for to preach the gospel unto them."

It was this verse as I stated earlier that the Lord used in calling me into the mission field. I was burdened and praying about going into Haiti to preach and the Lord gave me the assurance I needed that this is exactly what He wanted me and my family to do. We did deputation work for a while and made four mission trips there preaching the gospel with a group. We saw so many precious souls saved in these missionary journeys. On almost every trip, we saw a hundred or more souls saved in about a two week period of time. I praise the Lord for every opportunity that He gave us to preach the Gospel there and for every soul that was saved. Because of many circumstances that occurred, we were never able to go there and live, but the mission trips were what God wanted us to do at that time.

Paul and his mission team left Troas and went straight to Samothracia and the next day they came to Neapolis and from here they came to <u>Philippi, which was the chief city in Macedonia.</u> Paul tells us that they were in that city several days preaching. Thank God for Paul answering this call. Most of my ancestors came from Europe and here Paul is answering the call and preaching no doubt to some of my ancestors and hopefully many of them got saved. This, I believe, had a great deal to do with me being saved and preaching the gospel today.

DOWN BY THE RIVERSIDE

Acts 16:13 – 15 says, *"And on the sabbath we went out of the city by a river side, where prayer was wont to be made; and we sat down, and spake unto the women which resorted thither. And a certain woman named Lydia, a seller of purple, of the city of Thyatira, which worshipped God, heard us: whose heart the Lord opened, that she attended unto the things which were spoken of Paul. And when she was baptized, and her household, she besought us, saying, If ye have judged me to be faithful to the Lord, come into my house, and abide there. And she constrained us."*

It was from Philippi that they traveled out of the city on the sabbath and found a prayer meeting in a most unusual place, down by a river side. Paul and his team sat down with these women at the prayer meeting and began to speak to them. As they spoke there was a certain woman whose name was Lydia who heard them. When you preach or share the gospel message with people, you never know who might be listening to what you have to say. Lydia was a seller of purple from the city of Thyatira and she worshipped God. As she listened to them speak that day, the Lord opened her heart and she believed the things that were being said by Paul and got saved that day. Lydia was the first convert on their second missionary journey. She was so overcome by her new found faith that she was baptized there at the river and all of her household. This simply indicates that her family believed and were saved as well as Lydia and were baptized the same time she was.

Lydia then desires to have these men of God to come to her house and abide there. She uses the persuasion *"If ye have judged me to be faithful"* meaning that if you believe that I really got saved, then let me do this to show my sincerity for what you have done. She no doubt had plans to feed them and give them rest from their labors in Macedonia. One thing we should note in verse 15 is the last part where it says, *"And she constrained us."* Notice the word here "us". This was all the men of God that was with Paul at this point in his journey, which was Paul himself, Silas, Timothy and Luke. She "constrained" them to go, which means that she compelled or obliged them to go with her.

* What 2 places were Paul and Silas forbidden to preach?

1.   **2.**

* What does this show us about their ministry?

* Why did he forbid them to preach?

* What 2 things must be done in the missionary's life?
  1.
  2.

* What happened to Paul at Troas?

* What did he see and hear?

* What did they do immediately after this?

* What was the chief city of Macedonia?

* What did they find outside of Philippi on the Sabbath?

* What happened to Lydia at the prayer meeting?

* What else happened to Lydia that day?

Lesson Five:
Deliverance and Prison

DELIVERANCE OF DAMSEL POSSESSED WITH A SPIRIT OF DIVINATION

Acts 16:16 – 22 says, *"And it came to pass, as we went to prayer, a certain damsel possessed with a spirit of divination met us, which brought her masters much gain by soothsaying: The same followed Paul and us, and cried, saying, These men are the servants of the most high God, which shew unto us the way of salvation. And this did she many days. But Paul, being grieved, turned and said to the spirit, I command thee in the name of Jesus Christ to come out of her. And he came out the same hour. And when her masters saw that the hope of their gains was gone, they caught Paul and Silas, and drew them into the marketplace unto the rulers, And brought them to the magistrates, saying, These men, being Jews, do exceedingly trouble our city, And teach customs, which are not lawful for us to receive, neither to observe, being Romans. And the multitude rose up together against them: and the magistrates rent off their clothes, and commanded to beat them."*

Prayer was an important part of the life of Paul and those with him. We see them here again, going to pray. This should be a regular practice for the child of God. Notice when they came upon a prayer meeting by the river side, Lydia and her household were saved. Now they are coming to prayer and a certain damsel possessed with a spirit of divination met them, day after day. Her masters made a lot of money from her soothsaying. This lady is possessed by a devil and yet she has enough insight to say of Paul, Silas, Timothy and Luke in verse 17 that *"These men are the*

_____ *of the most high* _____, *which shew*

unto _____ *the way of* _____." She recognized the power of God working through them.

The Scripture tells us that she did this many days. Day after day as they were headed down to pray, this young lady would cry out as they passed by and Paul finally had enough as being grieved he turned and said to the spirit, *"I command thee in the name of Jesus Christ to come out of her. And he came out of her that same hour."* Dr. Sightler said, "<u>the method I employ in casting out devils is to turn the light on, the light of the Gospel.</u> When I preach the Gospel of the grace of God, the devils take leave and the devils flee because they despise the light, their deeds being evil." He further says, "Preachers and evangelist in our day have no apostolic authority to cast out devils as did Paul in this chapter."

When her masters saw what was done and that she had no more evil spirit in her to make money for them, they caught Paul and Silas and drew them into the marketplace to the rulers and magistrates and accused them. They said to them, "<u>*These men, being Jews, do exceedingly trouble our city,*</u> *and teach customs, which are not lawful for us to receive or to observe because we are Romans."* Notice the accusation is against who they are, Jews. This is definitely an anti-Semitic spirit. The people are persecuting them for being Jews, for being a part of the people of Israel. They accuse them of teaching things that they ought not, but again all they are doing is preaching the Gospel.

The multitude then rose up against Paul and Silas and the magistrates strip off their clothes and commanded them to be beaten. Paul and Silas did not deserve the punishment they were receiving. The only thing they had done was cast the devil out of this young lady and caused her masters to lose what money they were making from her.

PAUL AND SILAS BEATEN AND THROWN IN PRISON

Acts 16:23 – 34 tells us, *"And when they had laid many stripes upon them, they cast them into prison, charging the jailor to keep them safely: Who, having received such a charge, thrust them into the inner prison, and made their feet fast in the stocks. And at midnight Paul and Silas prayed, and sang praises unto God: and the prisoners heard them. And suddenly there was a great earthquake, so that the foundations of the prison were shaken: and immediately all the doors were opened, and every one's bands were loosed. And the keeper of the prison awaking out of his sleep, and seeing the prison doors open, he drew out his sword, and would have killed himself, supposing that the prisoners had been fled. But Paul cried with a loud voice, saying, Do thyself no harm: for we are all here. Then he called for a light, and sprang in, and came trembling, and fell down before Paul and Silas, And brought them out, and said, Sirs, what must I do to be saved? And they said, Believe on the Lord Jesus Christ, and thou shalt be saved, and thy house. And they spake unto him the word of the Lord, and to all that were in his house. And he took them the same hour of the night, and washed their stripes; and was baptized, he and all his, straightway. And when he had brought them into his house, he set meat before them, and rejoiced, believing in God with all his house."*

Along with the beating, which the Scripture refers to as "many stripes", they are then cast into prison. They are placed in charge of the jailer, who places them into the inner prison. Here are the two men of God, Paul and Silas, trying to follow the leading of the Holy Spirit, preaching the Word of God and doing the will of the Lord and yet they find themselves locked up in prison. Yes, bad things do happen to the children of God, but God has a way of turning the bad that happens in our lives into something good. He knows just how to use everything that happens to us to fulfill His will. Romans 8:28 says,

"And we _____ that all things _____

_____ for _____ to them that love

_____, to them who are the _____ according to

his _____."

So with the charge against them of troubling the city, sowing discord and disturbing the public peace, they are beaten and cast into the inner prison for punishment. Remember it was Ahab that said to Elijah in 1 Kings 18:17, *"Art thou he that troubleth Israel."* Oh that we, as Christians, could trouble our cities and towns where we live." This troubling was the stirring of the message in the souls of men who would not hear. The shaking of the people that would have brought them peace forever, but they refused. Through our message and testimony many are troubled every day. God is working in their hearts and wanting them to receive the free gift He has for them through the grace given by Jesus Christ.

They are now in the "inner prison" which is the dungeon. A dark, damp, dreary place where only the worst criminals were placed. No doubt he thought that he could keep them from escaping if they were keep here. He put their feet in the stocks and locked them in. Here lies two men of God that have been wrongly accused, beaten with many stripes, suffering this punishment for the cause of Christ. Remember earlier when we mentioned the prayer life of Paul and Silas. Well that has not changed. These men prayed about everything. Verse 25 tells us that

"At _____ Paul and Silas _____

and sang _____ unto _____." They were not praying at an hour of prayer or in the house of prayer, but in a dungeon. There is no place or time when it is not a good time to pray!

Their hearts overflowed with the joy of their prayer. Wouldn't you like to have that prayer recorded in the scriptures? What did they say? What was their petition? Whatever it was, it stirred their hearts and here lying on a cold damp floor in pain and agony these men worshipped God. They may have been locked away, but God was right there with them. They felt His presence as they cried out to Him! Their hearts were so full of praise that they begin to sing. Oh what a time a worship these men had!

* **What method did Dr. Sightler say that he used to cast out devils?**

* When Paul and Silas are brought before the magistrates and rulers, what accusation is made against them?

* What was done to Paul and Silas?

* At midnight, what did Paul and Silas do?

Lesson Six:
Revival Breaks out in Prison

But then something happened! Locked away in the innermost part of the prison, <u>the other prisoners heard them</u>. I believe they listened, many in unbelief and others wanting and longing for what these men of God had. Then another miracle happened. <u>A great earthquake</u> began to shake the prison and the very foundation of the prison was shaken. And immediately <u>all the doors of the prison were opened and every one's bands were loosed</u>. God heard their prayer and God sent deliverance.

The keeper of the prison was so sure that there was no way that any of these prisoners could ever escape, went to sleep. Probably the shaking of the earthquake and the sound of their chains falling off, along with the sound of the creaky doors of the prison being opened had awakened him. I believe that he was standing guard and then sleeping, just outside the door of the inner prison where Paul and Silas were being kept. When he woke up, he saw what had happened and supposing that everyone had escaped, drew out his sword to kill himself. The charge of the prisoners was on this jailer and <u>if just one of the prisoners had escaped, it would mean the life of the jailer would be taken</u>. He decided to miss all that and just go ahead and take his own life. But Paul cried out to him and said, *"Do thyself no harm: for we are all here."*

The jailer called for a light, remember it is so dark that you can't see your hand in front of your face, and then he ran in to where Paul and Silas were. There trembling, he fell down before them and the first thing he asked was *"Sirs, what must I do to be saved?"* They answered him by saying, *"Believe on the Lord Jesus Christ, and thou shalt be saved, and thy house."* Then they spoke unto him the Word of the Lord and to all those of his house.

The keeper of the prison took them out of the prison and washed their stripes and then he and his whole household were baptized. That means that that got saved from hearing the message of Christ from Paul and Silas. The jailer then set them down and fed them all the while he was rejoicing, because he had put his trust in Christ. *"Believing in God with all his house."*

Though Paul and Silas were imprisoned and suffered wrongfully, the Lord worked it all out for His good and His glory. The jailers and his household got saved. Though that is all that Luke recorded about the events of that night, I believe that there were many of the prisoners, if not all of them, that got saved that night. I say that because when the opportunity for the prisoners to leave was provided, none of them left their cell. God knows what He is doing in every situation of life. All we need to do is just trust Him and continue to serve Him.

PAUL AND SILAS LEFT PRISON - GO TO HOUSE OF LYDIA - THEN DEPART

Acts 16:35 – 40 says, *"And when it was day, the magistrates sent the serjeants, saying, Let those men go. And the keeper of the prison told this saying to Paul, The magistrates have sent to let you go: now therefore depart, and go in peace. But Paul said unto them, They have beaten us openly uncondemned, being Romans, and have cast us into prison; and now do they thrust us out privily? nay verily; but let them come themselves and fetch us out. And the serjeants told these words unto the magistrates: and they feared, when they heard that they were Romans. And they came and besought them, and brought them out, and desired them to depart out of the city. And they went out of the prison, and entered into the house of Lydia: and when they had seen the brethren, they comforted them, and departed."*

As soon as it was morning, the magistrates sent orders to let Paul and Silas go. Remember the magistrates had them beaten with many stripes publicly the day before. Now these same men that had beaten them are sent down to set them free. The jailer immediately tells Paul and Silas the news, "The magistrates have sent to let you go, therefore depart, and go in peace." Paul replies that they were beaten publicly and cast into prison and he mentions that they were Romans. He tells the serjeants that if they want them out they will have to come and get them out themselves. The serjeants convey the message to the magistrates and immediately, fear grips their heart in hearing that they were Romans. Matthew Henry says that "Roman historians give instances of cities that had their charters taken from them for indignities done to Roman citizens. Paul uses this later in Acts 22:25, 26. It did not bother them that they had beaten and imprisoned the servants of Christ. But fear filled their hearts to hear that they had done that to Roman citizens. They feared that someone would tell the government what they had done.

Paul refuses to leave until they acknowledge their injustice publicly. Then they came down themselves and brought them out of the prison and at the same time desired that they would depart out of the city. They left the prison and <u>went to the house of Lydia</u> where they knew they would be welcome. They had a final visit with the brethren, comforted them and then departed.

Paul and Silas had come to Philippi with a call and a burden, yet they saw little fruit of their labors and are now driven out of town. But they did not preach there in vain. Besides the account of Lydia and her household and the jailer and his household there was much sowing of seed in this place. Though they may not see it now, later they will see what great things they have done. <u>The foundation of the church at Philippi was laid</u>. The harvest shall come in due time.

* **What else happened when Paul and Silas prayed and sang praises?**

* **What other miracle took place that night?**

* **When the prison was shaken, what happen then?**

* **Why was the jailer going to kill himself?**

* When he came and fell down before Paul and Silas, what did he ask them?

* What was their answer?

* Where did they go when they were released from prison?

* What had Paul and Silas done in preaching in Philippi?

Lesson Seven:
Next Stop Thessalonica

Acts 17:1 – 4 says, *"Now when they had passed through Amphipolis and Apollonia, they came to Thessalonica, where was a synagogue of the Jews: And Paul, as his manner was, went in unto them, and three sabbath days reasoned with them out of the scriptures, Opening and alleging, that Christ must needs have suffered, and risen again from the dead; and that this Jesus, whom I preach unto you, is Christ. And some of them believed, and consorted with Paul and Silas; and of the devout Greeks a great multitude, and of the chief women not a few."*

Paul and Silas continue on in preaching the Word despite the treatment they receive in Philippi. He mentions this in his first letter to them in 1 Thessalonians 2:2 *"After we*

were _____ treated at _____, yet we

were _____ in our God to _____ unto you the

_____ of God." The persecution and opposition that they met only <u>made them more determined to get the gospel message out</u>. That should be our desire. There will be those that will treat us in a bad way, but don't let that stop you from telling someone else about Christ.

<u>Missions is not easy, but it's necessary</u>. In His commission, He didn't say everyone would be receptive to the message, He only told us to go and tell them. He didn't say that people would love you because you told them the

gospel message, but He did say go! At whatever the cost, Paul and Silas preached the word faithfully in every city and town they went into. We must be faithful in our witness.

Thessalonica was the chief city of this country. We're told that he only passed through Amphipolis which was a city near Philippi and Apollonia which was a city of Illyricum, near Thessalonica. Romans 15:19 says, *"Through*

mighty _____ *and* _____ *, by the*

_____ *of the* _____ *of God; so that from*

_____ *, and round about unto* _____ *,*

I have fully _____ *the* _____ *of*

Christ." This indicates that in passing through these cities, He also took the time to preach the Gospel there.

In Thessalonica, he preach the gospel to the Jews first. Then for three sabbath days reasoned with them out of the scriptures. Notice how he reasoned, not from something he had been told nor from some thought someone had told him about Christ, but *"out of the scriptures."* He told them how that Christ *"must needs have suffered and risen again from the dead"* and then told them that this Jesus that he was preaching about was Christ or the Messiah. Most of the Jews had a hard time understanding the suffering of Christ. Paul explains it was for us, for all men. He explains to them that Christ had to die in order to be resurrected for us.

The success of these three sabbath meetings was that

"*some of them believed*". Not only did they believe but they "*consorted with Paul and Silas.*" A great multitude believed, yet there is no mention of the Gentile idolaters being preached to or getting saved. Yet we know that they did from Paul's letter to the church at Thessalonica in 1 Thess. 1:9 where he said, "*For they themselves shew of us what*

_____ *of* _____ *in we had unto you,*

and how ye _____ *to* _____ *from* _____

to _____ *the* _____ *and* _____ *God;"*

Acts 17:5 – 9 says, "*But the Jews which believed not, moved with envy, took unto them certain lewd fellows of the baser sort, and gathered a company, and set all the city on an uproar, and assaulted the house of Jason, and sought to bring them out to the people. And when they found them not, they drew Jason and certain brethren unto the rulers of the city, crying, These that have turned the world upside down are come hither also; Whom Jason hath received: and these all do contrary to the decrees of Caesar, saying that there is another king, one Jesus. And they troubled the people and the rulers of the city, when they heard these things.*"

In verse 5 we see the trouble that came from the great success of Paul and Silas in preaching the gospel and seeing so many saved. Wherever Paul and Silas preached they were sure to face opposition and persecution. They knew it was coming, but they preached anyhow. They were on a mission to tell people everywhere they went of the saving grace of Jesus. We are told here that the troublemakers were "*the Jews who believed not*" and notice they were "*moved with envy*". The Jews were usually the greatest enemies of Christianity. Paul mentioned this rage of the Jews in 1 Thess. 2: 15, 16 where

he said, *"Who both _____ the Lord Jesus, and their*

_____ prophets, and have _____ us; and

they _____ not God, and are _____

to all men: Forbidding us to _____ to the _____

that they might be _____, to fill up their sins alway: for

the _____ is come upon them to the _____."

These Jews are said to have used certain lewd fellows of the baser sort. All the people who were wise treated Paul and Silas with respect, but this company of wicked men were glad to stand against them. Isn't it interesting that many times the troublemakers are the ones who just don't understand what Christianity is all about! These wicked, vile men are said to have *"set the city on an uproar."* They basically started a riot. Matthew Henry says this is the way the devil carries on his designs: "he sets cities in an uproar, sets souls in an uproar, and then fishes in troubled waters." They assaulted the house of Jason, hoping to bring them out and no doubt pull them to pieces but they could not find them.

Since they could not find Paul and Silas, they drew Jason out of his house and certain other brethren and brought them before the rulers of the city. Their accusation against them was *"These that have turned the world upside down are come hither also."* What an accusation! They are being accused of turning the world upside down. If you will be honest, that is exactly what happened when you got saved. Jesus coming into your heart rooted out the sin and washed it away! The way of the world that we were so accustomed to was turned upside down and we were a better people because of it. Actually, they were meaning to cause more trouble by this accusation, but they are telling the truth of what really happens when a person gets saved.

Another thought about this statement is that oh, that that could be made against us as believers today! That people would say about us, that we are turning the world upside down. Taking the message of the Gospel to a sinful people in love with the world and seeing them cleansed and walking away from the life style they once had in the world. They turn their accusations against Jason now saying that he has believed these men.

In verse seven they give <u>another accusation</u> which is that "<u>*these all do contrary to the decrees of Ceasar.*</u>" They are not suggesting a certain law that was made, for there were none against Christianity, but they were saying they were against Ceasar's power. Notice they said, that Paul and Silas were preaching about another king, one Jesus. When Peter preached his first message to the Gentiles in Acts 10:36 he said, "*The word which God sent unto the children of Israel, preaching peace by Jesus Christ: (he is Lord of all:)*" The accusation carried no real force for Christ's kingdom was not of this world. They did not understand that when the Christians referred to Jesus as a King, they were not talking about one who was rival of Ceasar. Jesus even taught for men to "*render unto Ceasar the things that are Ceasar's.*"

The result of the accusations was that *"they troubled the people and the rulers of the city."* When they heard that Paul and Silas were against Ceasar, they were troubled. They feared what might happen to them because of believing in and following the teaching of such men. Their hearts of both the people and the rulers of the city were troubled.

* What did the persecution and opposition in Philippi cause Paul and Silas to do?

* Missions is not _____ , but it is _____.

* What does Romans 15:19 indicate about Paul and Silas "passing through" some cities where there is no mention of preaching or conversions?

* How did Paul reason with those in Thessalonica in the synagogue?

* What was the result of these three Sabbath meetings they held?

* Wherever Paul and Silas preached, what were they sure to face?

* In Acts 17:5, who are the troublemakers?

* Who were usually the greatest enemies of Christianity?

* When they brought Jason out, what 2 accusations were made against Paul and Silas?
  1.
  2.

Lesson Eight:
Paul and Silas sent to Berea

PAUL SENT TO ATHENS, SILAS AND TIMOTHY REMAIN IN BEREA

Acts 17:10 – 15 says, "*And the brethren* _____

sent away Paul and Silas by night unto _____: *who*

coming thither went into the _____ *of*

the _____. *These were more* _____ *than those*

in Thessalonica, in that they _____ *the word with all*

_____ *of mind, and* _____

the scriptures _____, *whether those things were so.*

Therefore many of them _____; *also of*

_____ *women which were Greeks, and of*

men, not a few. But when the _____ *of Thessalonica had*

_____ *that the* _____ *of God was*

_____ *of Paul at Berea, they came thither*

also, and _____ up the people. And then

immediately the _____ sent away _____ to

go as it were to the sea: but _____ and _____

abode there still. And they that conducted Paul brought him unto

_____: and receiving a commandment unto Silas and

Timotheus for to _____ to him with all speed, they

departed."

The brethren, recognizing the danger that Paul and Silas were in, sent them by night to Berea. The first place they went to when they came into Berea was the Jewish synagogue. Dr. Sightler says the first place they always went was to the Jews. There are reasons for that he says. One of the reasons is because <u>there were no Baptist churches or any other kind of churches</u>, because the new church is now being founded upon the earth. Paul being a believer, went into the synagogue, <u>for he was a Jew of the tribe of Benjamin, a Hebrew of the Hebrews</u>. We are told that <u>these were more noble than those in Thessalonica</u> and the thing that made them this way was that <u>they received the word with all readiness of mind and they searched the scriptures daily to see if what they were being taught and preached was the truth.</u>

The people in Berea were more willing to listen to the preaching of Paul and Silas. They searched the scriptures to make sure they were being told the truth. They had an open mind to the word of God. Because of their willingness to search the scripture, <u>they were more likely to find the truth that leads to eternal life</u>. Dr. Sightler tells the story of the man who wrote the book Ben Hur, a man by the name of Lou Wallace. He was a Jew and when he began writing the book he was not a believer. But through all the daily research and reading and searching he did, by the time he had finished the book, he was a believer. "There is something about the Bible. It is the dynamite of God. It is the power of God unto salvation. The Bible is a living book; and when men read it, when men hear it, something happens, as surely as you live." *Dr. Sightler*

Because of their willingness to search the scriptures and listen as these men of God preached, verse 12 tells us than <u>many of them believed</u>. They were persuaded by the word of God that they needed Jesus and they repented and received Him as their Savior. We are told that many honorable women which were Greeks were saved and a good number of the men.

I always think when I come to this portion of Scripture, why those unbelieving Jews of Thessalonica never had any interest in those of Berea until they got saved. As soon as they knew about the great number of men and women that had been saved, they came to Berea with the sole purpose of stirring up the people. There will always be some who believe that their destiny on earth is to stir up some kind of trouble when God begins to move. This time the brethren in Berea send Paul away by sea. We are told that <u>Silas and Timothy remain there in Berea. Paul is brought by ship to Athens</u> where he immediately sends for Silas and Timothy to come to Athens as soon as they can get there. 1 Thess. 3:1, 2 tells us that Timothy was sent to Thessalonica to check on their affairs and give a report to Paul. The Scripture here says, *"Wherefore when we could no longer forbear, we thought it good to be left at Athens alone; And sent Timotheus, our brother, and minister of God, and our fellowlabourer in the gospel of Christ, to establish you, and to comfort you concerning your faith:"*

  * **Why was the synagogue the first place that Paul and Silas usually went?**
    1.
    2.

  * **What is said about those in Berea?**

  * **Why was this said of them?**

  * **What does their willingness to search the Scripture provide?**

  * **What does verse 12 tell us the result were?**

  * **Silas and Timothy remain in _____.**

  * **Paul is brought by ship to _____.**

Lesson Nine:
Paul Alone At Athens

Acts 17:16 – 34 says, "*Now while Paul waited for them at Athens, his spirit was stirred in him, when he saw the city wholly given to idolatry. Therefore disputed he in the synagogue with the Jews, and with the devout persons, and in the market daily with them that met with him. Then certain philosophers of the Epicureans, and of the Stoicks, encountered him. And some said, What will this babbler say? other some, He seemeth to be a setter forth of strange gods: because he preached unto them Jesus, and the resurrection. And they took him, and brought him unto Areopagus, saying, May we know what this new doctrine, whereof thou speakest, is? For thou bringest certain strange things to our ears: we would know therefore what these things mean. (For all the Athenians and strangers which were there spent their time in nothing else, but either to tell, or to hear some new thing.) Then Paul stood in the midst of Mars' hill, and said, Ye men of Athens, I perceive that in all things ye are too superstitious. For as I passed by, and beheld your devotions, I found an altar with this inscription, TO THE UNKNOWN GOD. Whom therefore ye ignorantly worship, him declare I unto you. God that made the world and all things therein, seeing that he is Lord of heaven and earth, dwelleth not in temples made with hands; Neither is worshipped with men's hands, as though he needed any thing, seeing he giveth to all life, and breath, and all things; And hath made of one blood all nations of men for to dwell on all the face of the earth, and hath determined the times before appointed, and the bounds of their habitation; That they should seek the Lord, if haply they might feel after him, and find him, though he be not far from*

every one of us: For in him we live, and move, and have our being;
as certain also of your own poets have said, For we are also his
offspring. Forasmuch then as we are the offspring of God, we ought
not to think that the Godhead is like unto gold, or silver, or stone,
graven by art and man's device. And the times of this ignorance
God winked at; but now commandeth all men every where to
repent: Because he hath appointed a day, in the which he will judge
the world in righteousness by that man whom he hath ordained;
whereof he hath given assurance unto all men, in that he hath
raised him from the dead. And when they heard of the resurrection
of the dead, some mocked: and others said, We will hear thee again
of this matter. So Paul departed from among them. Howbeit
certain men clave unto him, and believed: among the which was
Dionysius the Areopagite, and a woman named Damaris, and
others with them."

The first impression that Paul has of Athens while he
awaits the arrival of Silas and Timothy is expressed in the
words "*his spirit was stirred in him, when he saw the city wholly*
given to idolatry." Paul was not impressed at being in the
great city of philosophy and learning. All he sees is a people
that have replaced God with so many idols that they don't
even know the true and living God. Therefore, he disputes
with them about their condition. Remember Paul's mission
wherever he is at is to preach the gospel message to those
who are lost. He disputes (to engage in argument or debate)
with the Jews in the synagogue, with the devout persons,
(those showing deep religious feeling or commitment), with
those in the market and those he meets along the way and he
does it on a daily basis.

In verse 18 we are introduced to a group of philosophers
who were of the Epicureans. The Epicureans, according to

Matthew Henry, were a group that viewed God as one as themselves, an idle inactive being, that did not put any difference between good and evil. They would not own, either that God made the world or that he governs it; not that man needs to make any conscience of what he says or does, having no punishment to fear nor rewards to hope for. The Epicureans indulged themselves in all the pleasures of sense, and placed their happiness in them.

We are also introduced to <u>the Stoicks</u> who thought themselves to be as good as God and indulged themselves as much in the pride of life as the Epicureans did in the lusts of the flesh and of the eye. They taught contrary to Christianity which teaches us to deny ourselves and abase ourselves . . . that Christ may be all in all. These are the beliefs and lifestyles of these groups that *"encountered him"*.

Many of these groups thought Paul to be a fool. They called him a babbler. *"What will this babbler say?"* The word "babbler" used by these philosophers meant <u>"that he retailed odds and ends of knowledge which he had picked up from others, without possessing himself any system of thought or skill of language--without culture."</u> Basically they were accusing him of doing what they were doing.

They also accused him of be a *"setter forth of strange gods"*. <u>This was because he had preached Jesus unto them and his resurrection.</u> Though the philosophers in Athens were constantly seeking knowledge and were always interested in learning some new thing, the preaching and teaching of Paul concerning Jesus and His resurrection baffled them and they looked upon it as a strange doctrine.

They were so interested in knowing more about this Jesus and His resurrection that they brought Paul unto Areopagus or Mars Hill so that they might hear more about this new doctrine as they called it. They were interested in knowing what this doctrine was all about.

Paul then stood in the midst of Mars hill and said to those gathered there, "Ye men of Athens, I perceive that in all things ye are too superstitious." He states the reason for saying this to them was because of the devotion they had to the many idols throughout the city. They had an idol for every god they could think of so as not to offend any of them.

The term "too superstitious" refers to a belief or practice resulting from ignorance, fear of the unknown, trust in magic or chance, or a false conception of causation. The idols that were everywhere in Athens was a good indicator. People today are altogether too superstitious and most of it comes from things we have been taught all our lives about what to do if a certain thing happens. But most of our "superstitions" come from a **lack of** knowledge of the Word of God. Knowing what God says and knowing what God has done with sin through His Son on Calvary helps to do away with a superstitious mind.

Some of the superstitions of today have been handed down for generations. Some of them are: Throwing salt over your shoulder, a black cat crossing your path, stepping on a crack, opening an umbrella indoors, a broken mirror, knocking on wood, a rabbits foot, a horseshoe, crossing your fingers, saying bless you when someone sneezes, sweeping under your feet, failing to respond to a chain letter, walking under a ladder, and many more! All of these, we have been told will either bring us luck or ward off evil spirits or bad luck from our lives. The truth is that none of them are true. If you are not completely sure, check with the Old King James Bible and see if you can find any truth to these old wives tales and superstitions that have been taught to us all our lives.

Paul, in continuing his message, says that he found and altar that was set up "TO THE UNKNOWN GOD." That was just in case they had ignorantly forgotten one or left one off so that would cover all their bases in their so called worship. Paul then begins his message here using this altar that was set up to the Unknown God. He tells them that though they are ignorant of this God, *"Him declare I unto you."*

Keep in mind that Paul is preaching the Gospel message here to heathen people. Those that do not know the true and living God and that are currently worshipping idols to gods that are not real. In teaching them what they were inquiring about it was necessary for Paul to lay a foundation. He tells them that His God is the One who created all things; that created the world and being the Lord of heaven of earth, needed no to dwell in temples made by men. He says that God is not worshipped by men's hands, for God has given to every man, life and breath and all things. God has created and is concerned with the lives of all men. He has set bounds for their habitation.

He then says, in verse 27, *"That they should seek the Lord, if haply they might feel after him, and find him, though he be not far from every one of us:"* Paul is telling them that God is everywhere present and He has his eye on us at all times and knows us better than we know ourselves. He is near you, yet because of unbelief, so far away from you. He continues is message by telling them that it is in him we live and move and have our being. He is saying that we have a necessary dependence on Him. He uses the saying that <u>we are His offspring, which refers to the fact we are formed by Him, formed for him and have more care from Him than and parent has ever cared for their child.</u>

Because we are His offspring, we ought not to think of the Godhead as an idol, made of gold or silver or stone carved out by some man's hand. Paul then turns his message toward an invitation where he preaches to them that God commandeth that all men everywhere repent. There will be a day of judgment he says when God will judge the world in Righteousness, by the one He has ordained, Jesus, and then he tells them that God gave the assurance to men by raising Him from the dead.

As he mentions the resurrection, <u>some of them mocked him</u>. Others said to him, <u>we will hear thee again concerning what you have said</u>. Then there were also <u>those who clave to him and believed</u>. That is usually the way a message on Jesus will turn out. Some will mock in unbelief; others will say, that may be so, but we will have to hear more; and others will believe and want to know more about the Lord.

We are given some of those who clave to him here, "<u>Dionysius the Areopagite</u>, and a woman named <u>Damaris</u>, and others with them." Though the harvest at Athens was not as great as at other places Paul had been, he could not leave this place saying that he had labored here in vain.

* What was Paul's impression of Athens while he waited on Silas and Timothy?

* Who does Paul dispute with on a daily basis?
   1.
   2.
   3.
   4.

* What are the 2 groups of philosophers in Athens that encountered Paul?

* What does the word "babbler" mean here?

* Why did they accuse Paul of being a "setter forth of strange gods?"

* Where did they bring Paul to be able to hear more about his teachings?

* What did the term "too superstitious" mean?

* What did the inscription say on the altar Paul found?

* What did Paul tell them about this God?

* Paul is preaching the gospel here to _____ people.

* What did Paul mean when he said "we are his offspring?"

* What were the 3 different responses to Paul's message?
   1.
   2.
   3.

Lesson Ten:
Paul Goes to Corinth

Acts 18:1-6 says, *"After these things Paul departed from Athens, and came to Corinth; And found a certain Jew named Aquila, born in Pontus, lately come from Italy, with his wife Priscilla; (because that Claudius had commanded all Jews to depart from Rome:) and came unto them. And because he was of the same craft, he abode with them, and wrought: for by their occupation they were tentmakers. And he reasoned in the synagogue every sabbath, and persuaded the Jews and the Greeks. And when Silas and Timotheus were come from Macedonia, Paul was pressed in the spirit, and testified to the Jews that Jesus was Christ. And when they opposed themselves, and blasphemed, he shook his raiment, and said unto them, Your blood be upon your own heads; I am clean: from henceforth I will go unto the Gentiles."*

Though Paul's reception at Athens had not been with persecutions as he had faced in other places in dealing with the Jews where they has run him out of the city, yet the reception was cold. He departs from Athens on his own leaving the care of these new converts to Dionysius, and travels to Corinth. It is here at <u>Corinth, the chief city of Achaia,</u> a rich and splendid city, a seacoast village on the Aegean Sea, that Paul is instrumental in establishing a church.

It is at Corinth that Paul finds <u>a Jewish man named Aquila and his wife, Priscilla</u>. They had come here to Corinth because of Claudius, the Roman Caesar. He hated the Jews and expelled them from Rome until they were all gone. Aquila and Priscilla had to leave and came to Athens, Greece and from there had come up to Corinth. Isn't it amazing how God works in people's lives? Even though the persecution was bad and they had to leave their home, had it not been for this, Paul would never have been able to meet them and use them in the ministry. What a wonderful God we serve!

Paul, along with Priscilla and Aquila, were tent makers. So he worked with them while he was in Corinth. In these days tents were quite common. Dr. Sightler said, "The thought occurred to me, I wonder how and why and when Paul became interested in building tents. As far as I know, there is not ever the remotest suggestion in all Paul's epistles as to why and how he became involved in this craft. It could have well been his father was a tentmaker, or it could have been that he had a brother or somebody else in his family who might have been a tentmaker. It could have been his grandfather who might have been a tentmaker. For some reason, Paul learned the art. So far as I am concerned, Paul was not only a tentmaker; but he was a trained educated man, a man of renown who sat at the feet of Gamaliel. And yet he had this craft which he could always fall back on to make a livelihood."

Paul, in verse 4, is doing exactly what he has done in all the other cities he had visited. The first thing he does is find the synagogue and on the Sabbath day he goes here to persuade and reason and preach and proclaim a resurrected Savior. This he does every Sabbath without exception.

We see that Silas and Timothy once again join the team in

Corinth. They had stayed behind in Berea when Paul had to leave for his safety. Paul waited in Athens for them to join him, but they never came. Now they arrive from Berea and are ready to begin working here. The scripture tells us that when they came, Paul was "pressed in the spirit." This means that he was burdened in his heart and had a consuming desire to preach the gospel to the Corinthians. This is just what he did, we are told he testified to them that "Jesus was Christ". He tells them that the Jesus he is preaching was the Messiah.

The Jews would not readily believe this, but the Gentiles believed. "When they opposed themselves, and blasphemed" meaning when they contradicted in their lives what they put their faith in, Paul then shook his raiment and said, "Your blood be upon your own heads." The Jews and the Greeks had rejected the message of the resurrection of Jesus and the message that Jesus was the Messiah. Paul tells them that he has preached daily to them about Christ, yet they will not accept this truth, so he declares that he is clean from their blood. He had done what he was sent to do, but they would not have the message that was sent, so Paul again says here that he will go unto the Gentiles.

So many times when we preach or teach or tell others about Jesus, the message falls on ground where the seed is never going to grow. Time after time, we tell them and time after time they turn us away. This is the way Paul was feeling at this time. He had preached faithfully, but for the most part his message was falling on deaf ears. They would not accept the truth of what Paul was preaching, but he never gave up.

Acts 18:7 – 11 says, "*And he departed thence, and entered into a certain man's house, named Justus, one that worshipped God, whose house joined hard to the synagogue. And Crispus, the chief ruler of the synagogue, believed on the Lord with all his house; and many of the Corinthians hearing believed, and were baptized. Then spake the Lord to Paul in the night by a vision, Be not afraid, but speak, and hold not thy peace: For I am with thee, and no man shall set on thee to hurt thee: for I have much people in this city. And he continued there a year and six months, teaching the word of God among them.*"

Paul leaves the synagogue here because of the unbelieving Jews and comes to the house of a man by the name of Justus. It would seem that Justus, living close to the synagogue had opened his doors so that Paul could continue preaching the gospel. We are told that Justus worshipped God. He was not an idol worshipper, but he was a Gentile. His house being close to the synagogue made it possible for some from the synagogue to come in to the meeting Paul was having.

Paul had results here that he probably had not expected. We are told that Crispus, who was the chief ruler of the synagogue had come and heard the message and had believed on the Lord Jesus Christ. Not only had he gotten saved, but all his house had believed. Also there were many Corinthians who heard the message and believed and were baptized. God continues to bless Paul with converts even though the Jews at the synagogue had rejected his message.

Paul, then in a vision at night, is told by the Lord, "*Be not afraid, but speak, and hold not thy peace.*" Just keep on preaching the Word. Don't ever give up!

Preach on, don't give up, so many need to hear.
Preach on, Preach on, their faces never fear.
Preach on, take a stand, tell them what is right.
Preach on, Preach on, be faithful in the fight.

The Lord gave him a promise of protection. He needed not to fear man, because God had promised to be with him and shield him from wicked and ungodly attacks. We have a similar promise in our commission to take the gospel message to the lost in Matthew 28:20 "... *and, lo, I am with you alway, even unto the end of the world.*"

God was giving great victory to his servant Paul. People were getting saved. The Lord gave him a promise and also told him that He had much people in the city. Paul's journeys, up until now, have been moving at a pretty rapid pace. But, in Corinth, he stays here for a year and six months teaching the word of God among them. It was during this time that Paul won a great number of the people of Corinth to the Lord. It was here he built a church that we read more about in 1 and 2 Corinthians. He never gave up and God rewarded him with results. His faithfulness should teach us. Dr. Sightler says, "We ought to learn the lesson of consistency, the lesson of faithfulness, the lesson of doing what God wills we do, and being what God wills we be."

* What is the chief city of Achaia?

* Who does Paul find in Corinth?

* What were their occupations along with Paul?

* What is the first place Paul goes on the Sabbath day?

* Who once again joins the team in Corinth?

* What does it mean when we are told Paul was "pressed in the spirit"?

* When Paul leaves the synagogue in Acts 18:7 whose house did he come into?

* What were the results of this meeting?

* How long did Paul stay in Corinth?

* What 3 lessons should we learn from Paul's labors according to Dr. Sightler?
  1.
  2.
  3.

Lesson Eleven:
Paul Finishes the Journey

Acts 18:12 – 17 says, "*And when Gallio was the deputy of Achaia, the Jews made insurrection with one accord against Paul, and brought him to the judgment seat, Saying, This fellow persuadeth men to worship God contrary to the law. And when Paul was now about to open his mouth, Gallio said unto the Jews, If it were a matter of wrong or wicked lewdness, O ye Jews, reason would that I should bear with you: But if it be a question of words and names, and of your law, look ye to it; for I will be no judge of such matters. And he drave them from the judgment seat. Then all the Greeks took Sosthenes, the chief ruler of the synagogue, and beat him before the judgment seat. And Gallio cared for none of those things.*"

It is always just a matter of time before Paul faces persecution from unbelievers when he travels on his missionary journeys. We should learn a lesson here as well, that if we are faithful to preach and teach and tell others the truth of the gospel, we too will face

persecution. 2 Timothy 3:12 says, "*Yea, and all that will*

_____ _____ *in Christ* _____

_____ *suffer* _____.*" If you live a godly life before this lost world, you will suffer persecution. Get used to it. It's going to happen. When it does, don't quit doing what you are supposed to be doing. Keep on being faithful to the Lord.

Here we are introduced to one <u>Gallio who was the deputy of Achaia</u>. That means that he was <u>a judge in the city of Corinth</u>. It was during his time in office that the Jews made insurrection with one accord against Paul. <u>Insurrection is "a violent uprising against an authority."</u> They then brought him to the judgment seat and accused him of persuading men to worship God contrary to the law. Which statement was true! Paul's message was contrary to the law. He had a greater faith to teach. He had a message that was for all that would hear and receive to take of the water of eternal life freely.

As Paul has heard the accusations against him, he is about to defend himself when Gallio stops him and addresses the Jews that brought him there. He tells them that if the matter before him is one of wrong or lewdness, he would gladly hear it. But he tells them if it is something that has to do with their law, you take care of it. He tells them <u>that he will not judge in spiritual matters</u> and with that he ran them out from the judgment seat.

The Greeks then out of revenge, take <u>Sosthenes, who was the chief ruler of the synagogue and beat him before the judgment seat</u>. Then the scriptures tell us, "<u>*And Gallio cared for none of these things.*</u>" <u>In other words, Gallio allowed this to happen</u>. There was no reason for this to happen, but it did. Gallio was right in not judging Paul, but he is absolutely wrong for not stepping in and stopping this injustice against Sosthenes.

Acts 18:18 – 22, "*And Paul after this tarried there yet a good while, and then took his leave of the brethren, and sailed thence into Syria, and with him Priscilla and Aquila; having shorn his head in Cenchrea: for he had a vow. And he came to Ephesus, and left them there: but he himself entered into the synagogue, and reasoned with the Jews. When they desired him to tarry longer time with them, he consented not; But bade them farewell, saying, I must by all means keep this feast that cometh in Jerusalem: but I will return again unto you, if God will. And he sailed from Ephesus. And when he had landed at Caesarea, and gone up, and saluted the church, he went down to Antioch."*

Paul tarried yet a good while here and then left and sailed to Syria. He took Priscilla and Aquila with him. The reason for his head being shorn and the vow he made in Cenchrea is not known. Dr. Sightler says, "The only explanation I can give as to Paul's deed and Paul's conduct was his consuming compassion for his kinsmen according to the flesh, and his longing desire to reach them with the Gospel of the grace of God."

Paul then left this port city, Cenchrea and came to Ephesus. We are told that at Ephesus he left Priscilla and Aquila. Paul continued to reason with the Jews in the synagogue. They wanted him to stay longer, but he was determined to keep the feast in Jerusalem. He promises them that he will visit them again and then adds, *"if God will."* Matthew Henry says, "Our times are in God's hand; we purpose, but he disposes; and therefore we must make all our promises with submission to the will of God."

He sailed from Ephesus and landed in Caesarea and went up and saluted the church in Jerusalem. He was there only briefly. Then he went down to Antioch. Here at his home church he would again rehearse the mission journey and what had happened to his sending church. It no doubt was a refreshing time for Paul to be able to see his friends and brethren again.

And so ends the second missionary journey of Paul.

* **Who are we introduced to in Acts 18:12 and what was his position?**

* **What does "insurrection" mean?**

* **What does Gallio tell these Jews that brought Paul before him?**

* **Who is it that the Greeks then take and beat before the judgment seat?**

* **What was his office?**

* **What does it mean when it says, "And Gallio cared for none of these things"?**

* **Where did Paul leave Priscilla and Aquila?**

* **What phrase does Paul use in telling them at Ephesus, he will visit them again?**

How Can We Support and Send Out Missionaries?

I believe that missions is the heart beat of God. Therefore, missions should be one of the primary interest of the church. God will always bless a mission minded church. I saw that from pastoring for over 25 years. We were able, by faith, to support more missionaries than we had people coming to church. What a blessing to support missionaries that you know personally. There's actually a thrill of being able to know that missionary and his family and know that when they win a soul on the mission field, God will put that on our account, because we had helped send that missionary to preach the gospel.

I have found in my years as a pastor that the best way to introduce your church to missions is to allow them to see firsthand what a missionary does. We did this by having a missionary and his family come by the church and give a testimony, preach or show slides and tell about what it is like on the mission field winning souls to Jesus.

The best way to support missionaries is to be able to know the missionary and what they are doing or planning to do on the mission field. We had many come by the church and myself and the church became great friends and supporters of many of these missionaries through the years. To be able to know where your money is going and what it is doing for the cause of Christ is priceless.

Many churches across the country today use what is called Faith Promise Missions. It is a simple to understand program to support missions and missionaries that really works. Some attribute the beginning of Faith Promise Missions to Dr. A. B. Simpson. He claimed to have gotten it from the Bible. I agree!

Faith in dealing with our finances is just as important as having faith and applying it in any other area of our lives. If we give by faith, God will provide what we need in a marvelous way, both in giving to missions and in having what we need supplied along the way.

We will never be able to do a great work for the Lord without faith! In 2 Corinthians 10:15-16 says, *"Not boasting of things without our measure, that is, of other men's labours; but having hope, when your faith is increased, that we shall be enlarged by you according to our rule abundantly, To preach the gospel in the regions beyond you, and not to boast in another man's line of things made ready to our hand."*

Notice he tells us that "When your faith is increased" then "we shall be enlarged by you," the purpose, "to preach the gospel in the regions beyond you". What a picture of faith promise missions we see in these verses. They show us that as our faith increases, we will give more and that will cause the missionary to be supported to the place they can reach the field and even to the regions beyond.

In 2 Corinthians chapters 8 and 9, we see at least 8 Biblical principles that define faith promise mission giving. The first thing we must do if we are to be faithful, fruitful givers to faith promise missions is in verse 5, we must first give ourselves to the Lord.

This is the most important of all the principles we see in these two chapters. If we don't belong to the Lord, nothing we do is going to prosper. If we belong to him and have not given ourselves to him to use in His service, then we are not ready to give our money. We must be willing to give ourselves or we will never be willing to give our money!

2 Corinthians 8:5 says, "And this they did, not as we hoped, but first gave their own selves to the Lord, and unto us by the will of God."

How important it is that before we undertake a program for giving to missions, we first examine ourselves and see where we stand. Then completely and totally commit ourselves to the Lord. If we have yielding all of ourselves to Him, then we are ready to invest all that the Lord would have us to in giving to missions. Search your heart! What is your commitment level to the Lord today! He doesn't want part of you, He wants all of you! Give Him your all today!

The second principle that we must meet in our faith promise giving is in 2 Corinthians 9:6, 7, "But this I say, He which soweth sparingly shall reap also sparingly; and he which soweth bountifully shall reap also bountifully. Every man according as he purposeth in his heart, so let him give; not grudgingly, or of necessity: for God loveth a cheerful giver."

Our attitude concerning our giving must be cheerful. The way we give, whether sparingly or bountiful, demonstrates our desire to further the work of God.
2 Corinthians 8:3 says, "For to their power, I bear record, yea, and beyond their power, they were willing of themselves."

2 Corinthians 8:12 says, "For if there be first a willing mind, it is accepted according to that a man hath, and not according to that he hath not."

We must give out of our willingness to give and not out of duty. We must have a willing mind in giving and that will lead to a willing heart. We give because we want to see the work of the Lord continue and prosper. We give because we want to see souls saved and then discipled through the teaching of the Word of God. We give because we care about others and are willing to give to try to reach them and help them in the Lord.

In verse 2 of 2 Corinthians 8 we are told, *"How in a great trial of affliction the abundance of their joy and their deep poverty abounded unto the riches of their liberality."* Their giving by faith allowed them to give "beyond their power". We are to give out of our need rather than out of our excess. This is real sacrificial giving!

It is emphasized that every believer should be involved in giving by faith.
2 Corinthians 8: 7 says, *"Therefore, as ye abound in every thing, in faith, and utterance, and knowledge, and in all diligence, and in your love to us, see that ye abound in this grace also."* Paul show us in these two chapters that financing missions does not depend on having a lot of money, but on having a willing heart.

2 Cor. 8:1-7 *1. Moreover, brethren, we do you to wit of the grace of God bestowed on the churches of Macedonia; 2 How that in a great trial of affliction the abundance of their joy and their deep poverty abounded unto the riches of their liberality. 3 For to their power, I bear record, yea, and beyond their power they were willing of themselves; 4 Praying us with much intreaty that we would receive the gift, and take upon us the fellowship of the ministering to the saints. 5 And this they did, not as we hoped, but first gave their own selves to the Lord, and unto us by the will of God. 6 Insomuch that we desired Titus, that as he had begun, so he would*

also finish in you the same grace also. 7 Therefore, as ye abound in every thing, in faith, and utterance, and knowledge, and in all diligence, and in your love to us, see that ye abound in this grace also."

Faith Promise Giving is an offering that is over and above your local church support. It is a promise, by faith, to contribute a certain amount over a period of a year. It was given by faith. God will honor a "faith commitment" of a Christian by making His grace abound. Grace usually comes in one of three ways. 1. New opportunities, such as overtime, new job, extra job. 2. Discipline, meaning a change in your life-style. 3. Grace of Unusual circumstances, such as in response to prayer, God answers in an unexpected way.

Faith Promise Giving allows the Lord an opportunity to work in our lives to give to reach the lost.
Faith Promise Giving says, "by faith, I will give $ _____ each week, or month to the Lord for missionary work".
Faith Promise Giving is a means of us fulfilling the great commission.
Faith Promise Giving is a means of weekly consistent discipline on our part to support World Missions.
Faith Promise Giving is an extra gift that you would not be able to give apart from trusting God to provide it.

Paul teaches us in 2 Cor. 8 and 9 that Faith Promise giving is (8:2-4) going to be more than you can afford. It will follow a personal commitment of giving yourself to the Lord, (8:5). It is not a commandment, but a commitment (8:8). It is something that is previously promised (9:5). It is something you personally purpose to give (9:7). It is a gift that you can give cheerfully (9:7). It is a gift, by faith, that God will provide (9:8).

How can you get involved? I have listed a few things here that will help you.

First, you need to realize that, as a Christian, God has entrusted you with the Gospel message, (1 Thess. 2:4, *"But as we were allowed of God to be put in trust with the gospel, even so we speak; not as pleasing men, but God, which trieth our hearts."* Secondly, we are commanded to take this Gospel to those around us and into all the world, (Acts 1:8, *"But ye shall receive power, after that the Holy Ghost is come upon you: and ye shall be witnesses unto me both in Jerusalem, and in all Judea, and in Samaria, and unto the uttermost part of the earth."*

Pray about what God would have you to give and be faithful to give that on a regular basis. See how God will bless you in being involved in world missions and enjoy the blessing of giving to get the message of the Gospel to a lost and dying world. Why not pray about getting involved in Faith Promise Giving today?

Made in the USA
Coppell, TX
23 January 2024